EVERLASTING JOY

Janis

Every Blessing

Cidy.

Copyright © 2023 by Cindy Mackenzie

First paperback edition June 2023

Book design by Amazing_5Design

Photographs by Rev Colin Mackenzie

DEDICATION

To my husband Colin, we do so much together it only seemed right to use his wonderful skills as a photographer as well as a Pastor.

To my daughter Michelle who is also an author (look out for her books and novels under Shelly Mack Books), and Bruce my son who is also a photographer. My next book which is coming very soon will feature his photographs from Patagonia, Chile.

To my beautiful Granddaughters Olivia & Gracie, who when I watch them and see their faith as children it teaches me so much. Their childlike faith is simply - believe in God. They trust Him and pray believing. Granny loves you girls.

TABLE OF CONTENTS

ABIDE IN MY LOVE

SCRIPTURE: John 15:10–12 NIV

"If you keep my commands, you will remain in my love, just as I have kept my Father's commands and remain in his love. [11] I have told you this so that my joy may be in you and that your joy may be complete. [12] My command is this: Love each other as I have loved you."

DECLARATION:

Jesus calls us to keep his commandments and abide in his love, so that we can experience his joy and love others as he has loved us.

REFLECTION:

In this passage, Jesus is speaking to his disciples about the importance of obeying his commandments and abiding in his love. He emphasises that he has kept his Father's commandments and abides in his love, setting an example for his followers to do the same. Jesus' love for us is unconditional and it is through obeying his commandments that we can experience the fullness of his love and joy. And as we experience his love and joy, we are called to love others in the same way.

MOTIVATION:

As followers of Christ, we are called to abide in his love by obeying his commandments. We are not only called to experience his love and joy but to share it with others by loving them as he has loved us. This can be challenging at times, but with the help of the Holy Spirit, we can love others sacrificially, just as Jesus loved us.

PRAYER:

Dear God, help us to abide in your love by obeying your commandments. Fill us with your joy and love so that we can love others in the same way you have loved us. Help us to love sacrificially and unconditionally, just as you have loved us. May our lives reflect your love and grace. In Jesus' name, we pray, Amen.

MORE JOY IN HEAVEN

SCRIPTURE: Luke 15:7 NIV

"I tell you that in the same way there will be more rejoicing in heaven over one sinner who repents than over ninety-nine righteous persons who do not need to repent."

DECLARATION:

Heaven rejoices over one sinner who repents.

REFLECTION:

In this parable, Jesus shares the story of a shepherd who leaves his ninety-nine sheep to search for the one that is lost. When he finds the lost sheep, he rejoices and calls his friends and neighbour to celebrate with him. Jesus then makes the declaration in verse 7, highlighting that there is more joy in heaven over one sinner who repents than over ninety-nine righteous persons who need no repentance. This declaration reminds us of the immense joy that comes from repentance and turning back to God.

MOTIVATION:

As Christians, we are called to share the good news of the Gospel and to reach out to those who are lost. This verse reminds us that there is incredible joy in heaven when one sinner repents and turns to God. It motivates us to continue to share the message of salvation with others, knowing that the reward of a single soul turning to God is immeasurable. Over the years I have had the joy of leading several people to Christ. I love to share the gospel. May God give you daily opportunities to say a word of encouragement, to find a way to speak of Him so others may see Christ in you and want to know more.

PRAYER

Dear God, we thank you for the joy that comes from repentance and turning back to you. Help us to reach out to those who are lost and to share the message of salvation with them. Give us the motivation and strength to continue to share your love and grace with others, even when it feels difficult. May we be a part of the joy in heaven as we see those who were lost come back to you. In Jesus', we pray, Amen.

GIVE THANKS TO THE LORD

SCRIPTURE:

1 Chronicles 16:32-34 NIV

"Let the sea resound, and all that is in it; let the fields be jubilant, and everything in them! Let the trees of the forest sing, let them sing for joy before the Lord, for he comes to judge the earth. Give thanks to the Lord, for he is good; his love endures forever. "

DECLARATION:

We are called to give thanks to the Lord for his goodness and steadfast love that endures forever.

REFLECTION:

This passage is part of a song of thanksgiving that David composed when the ark of the covenant was brought to Jerusalem. The passage calls on all of creation to praise God, from the sea to the fields, to the trees of the forest. It reminds us that God is the creator of all things and that all of creation rejoices in his presence. The declaration in verse 34 reminds us to give thanks to the Lord for his goodness and steadfast love, which never ends.

MOTIVATION:

As we reflect on this passage, we are motivated to give thanks to the Lord for his goodness and love. We are reminded that all of creation is designed to praise God, and we too should offer our thanks and praise to him. In giving thanks, we also acknowledge our dependence on God and our gratitude for all that he has done for us.

PRAYER:

Dear God, we give thanks to you for your goodness and steadfast love that endures forever. We thank you for the beauty of creation and for the ways that you sustain us each day. Help us to remember to offer our thanks and praise to you in all circumstances, knowing that you are the creator of all things and the source of our strength and hope. May our lives reflect your goodness and love, and may we continue to give thanks to you in all that we do. In Jesus' name, we pray, Amen.

OVERJOYED

SCRIPTURE: Matthew 2:9-10 NIV

"After they had heard the king, they went on their way, and the star they had seen when it rose went ahead of them until it stopped over the place where the child was. When they saw the star, they were overjoyed."

9

DECLARATION:

The magi were overjoyed when they saw the star that led them to Jesus.

REFLECTION:

The magi had travelled a great distance to find the one who had been born king of the Jews. They had followed a special star, and when it stopped over the place where Jesus was, they were filled with joy. This passage reminds us that the journey to find Jesus may not always be easy, but the reward of finding him is worth it. The declaration of their joy shows us the depth of their faith and the joy that comes from finding the Messiah.

MOTIVATION:

As we reflect on this passage, we are motivated to seek Jesus with the same dedication and determination as the wise men. We are reminded that the journey may be challenging, but the reward of finding Jesus is worth it. We are also motivated to share the joy of our faith with others, just as the wise men shared their joy and worshiped Jesus when they found him.

PRAYER:

Dear God, we thank you for the gift of your Son, Jesus Christ, and for the joy that comes from knowing him. Help us to seek him with the same dedication and determination as the magi, even when the journey is challenging. May we be filled with joy when we find Jesus, and may we share that joy with others. Help us to worship and honour Jesus in all that we do, and may our lives reflect his love and grace. In Jesus' name, we pray, Amen.

DESIRE OF YOUR HEART

SCRIPTURE: Psalm 20:4-5 NIV

"May he give you the desire of your heart and make all your plans succeed. May we shout for joy over your victory and lift up our banners in the name of our God. May the Lord grant all your requests."

DECLARATION:

The psalmist prays that God would give us the desire of our hearts and for our plans to succeed.

REFLECTION:

In this passage, we see the psalmist praying for the success and victory of God's people. The declaration of the psalmist's prayer reminds us that God is interested in our desires and plans. It also shows us that God is able to make those plans succeed, and that he is the source of our victories.

MOTIVATION:

As we reflect on this passage, we are motivated to trust in God's ability to give us the desires of our hearts and for our plans to succeed. We are reminded that God is interested in our goals and aspirations, and that he is able to bring them to fruition. We are also motivated to rejoice in the victories that God brings, and to give him the credit for our successes.

PRAYER:

Dear God, we thank you for your interest in our desires and plans. We ask that you consider the desire of our hearts that our plans would glorify you. Help us to trust in your ability to bring our goals to fruition, and to give you the credit for our successes. May we rejoice in the victories that you bring and lift up our banners in the name of our God. May you grant all our requests, according to your will. In Jesus' name, we pray, Amen.

REJOICING COMES IN THE MORNING

SCRIPTURE: Psalm 30:4-5 NIV

"Sing praises to the Lord, you his faithful people; praise his holy name. For his anger lasts only a moment, but his favour lasts a lifetime. Weeping may stay for the night, but rejoicing comes in the morning."

DECLARATION:

The psalmist declares that weeping may stay for the night, but rejoicing comes in the morning.

REFLECTION:

This passage reminds us that life can be filled with both joy and sorrow. We may experience weeping and mourning, but the declaration of the psalmist assures us that rejoicing will come in the morning. We are reminded that God's favour lasts a lifetime, even when we experience hardship and pain. We can trust that God will bring us through our trials and that joy will come in due time.

MOTIVATION:

As we reflect on this passage, we are motivated to trust in God's timing and faithfulness. We are reminded that our weeping and mourning will not last forever, and that God will bring us through our trials. We are also motivated to sing praises to God, even in the midst of our pain, knowing that rejoicing will come in the morning.

PRAYER:

Dear God, we thank you for your faithfulness and the promise of joy that comes in the morning. Help us to trust in your timing, even when we are experiencing hardship and pain.

May we sing praises to your holy name, even in the midst of our weeping and mourning, knowing that rejoicing will come in due time. Give us the strength and perseverance to endure our trials, and the faith to trust in your goodness and mercy. In Jesus' name, we pray, Amen.

GOD OF HOPE

SCRIPTURE: Romans 15:13 NIV

"May the God of hope fill you with all joy and peace as you trust in him, so that you may overflow with hope by the power of the Holy Spirit."

DECLARATION:

The Apostle Paul declares that God is the God of hope and that he desires to fill us with joy, peace, and hope.

REFLECTION:

This passage reminds us that God is the source of our hope. We may face difficult circumstances and uncertain futures, but God is always with us, and he desires to fill us with hope by the power of the Holy Spirit. We are reminded that our hope is not in our own strength or abilities, but in God's power and faithfulness. We can trust in God's promises and rest in the knowledge that he will never leave us or forsake us.

MOTIVATION:

As we reflect on this passage, we are motivated to trust in God's power and faithfulness. We are reminded that our hope is not in ourselves, but in God's ability to fill us with joy, peace, and hope. We are also motivated to overflow with hope and share the good news of God's love and faithfulness with others.

PRAYER:

Dear God, we thank you for being the God of hope. We ask that you fill us with all joy and peace as we trust in you, so that we may overflow with hope by the power of the Holy Spirit. Help us to trust in your power and faithfulness, even when we face difficult circumstances and uncertain futures. Give us the strength and courage to share the good news of your love and faithfulness with others, so that they too may experience the hope that comes from knowing you. In Jesus' name, we pray, Amen.

I REMEMBER YOU

SCRIPTURE: Psalm 63:6-7 NIV

"On my bed, I remember you; I think of you through the watches of night. Because you are my help, I sing in the shadow of your wings."

DECLARATION:

The psalmist declares that even in the watches of the night, he remembers God, and because of God's help, he sings in the shadow of his wings.

REFLECTION:

This passage reminds us of the importance of remembering God in all circumstances, even in the quiet moments of the night. We are reminded that God is our help and our refuge, and that we can rest in the shadow of his wings. We can trust in God's faithfulness and goodness, even when we are facing difficult circumstances. The psalmist's declaration is a reminder that God is always with us, and that we can find comfort and strength in his presence.

MOTIVATION:

As we reflect on this passage, we are motivated to remember God in all circumstances. We are reminded that even when we feel stressed and overwhelmed, we can turn to God and find comfort and strength in his presence. We are also motivated to sing praises to God, knowing that he is our help and our refuge.

PRAYER:

Dear God, we thank you for your faithfulness and goodness. Help us to remember you in all circumstances, in times of trouble or sadness. May we find comfort and strength in your in your presence, and may we rest in the shadow of your wings. Give us the d strength to sing praises to you, even in the midst of our difficulties. We trust in your faithfulness and goodness, and we know that you are always with us. In Jesus' name, we pray, Amen.

THE FRUIT OF THE SPIRIT

SCRPTURE: Galatians 5:22-23 NIV

"But the fruit of the Spirit is love, joy, peace, patience, kindness, goodness, faithfulness, gentleness, and self-control. Against such things there is no law."

DECLARATION:

The Apostle Paul declares that the fruit of the Spirit includes love, joy, peace, patience, kindness, goodness, faithfulness, gentleness, and self-control. He also emphasises that there is no law against these things.

REFLECTION:

This passage reminds us that as believers in Christ, we are called to live by the Spirit and produce fruit that reflects God's character. We are reminded that the fruit of the Spirit is not something that we can produce on our own, but it is the result of the Holy Spirit working in us.

As we allow the Holy Spirit to work in our lives, we will begin to exhibit the qualities of love, joy, peace, patience, kindness, goodness, faithfulness, gentleness, and self-control.

MOTIVATION:

As we reflect on this passage, we are motivated to live by the Spirit and produce fruit that reflects God's character. We are reminded that we cannot produce this fruit on our own, but we must rely on the Holy Spirit to work in our lives. We are also motivated to pursue these qualities in our own lives, knowing that they are pleasing to God and beneficial to those around us.

PRAYER:

Dear God, we thank you for the Holy Spirit, who works in us to produce the fruit of the Spirit. Help us to live by the Spirit and by doing so you will produce the fruit that reflects your character. We ask that you cultivate in us love, joy peace, patience, kindness, goodness, faithfulness, gentleness, and self-control. Help us to pursue these qualities in our own lives, and may we be a blessing to those around us. In Jesus' name, we pray, Amen.

SING FOR JOY TO THE LORD

SCRIPTURE: Psalm 95:1-2 NIV

"Come, let us sing for joy to the Lord; Let us shout aloud to the rock of our salvation. Let us come before him with thanksgiving and extol him with music and song."

DECLARATION:

The Psalmist declares that we should come together and sing for joy to the Lord. We should shout aloud to the Rock of our salvation and come before Him with thanksgiving, extolling Him with music and song.

REFLECTION:

This passage reminds us of the importance of worshiping God with joy and thanksgiving. It is a call to gather together and lift our voices in praise to our Creator and Saviour. We are called to approach God with a heart of gratitude, acknowledging His goodness and faithfulness in our lives. As we sing praises to Him, we are reminded of His power and majesty, and we are filled with joy and hope.

MOTIVATION:

As we reflect on this passage, we are motivated to come before the Lord with joy and thanksgiving, lifting our voices in praise to Him. We are reminded of the power in worship and how it can change our perspective and fill us with hope and joy. We are also motivated to acknowledge God's goodness and faithfulness in our lives and to give Him the honour and praise He deserves.

PRAYER:

Dear God, we come before you today with thanksgiving and joy in our hearts. We lift our voices in praise to you, the Rock of our salvation. We acknowledge your goodness and faithfulness in our lives, and we extol you with music and song. Help us to always remember the power in worship and to come before you with a heart of gratitude. May our worship be a pleasing aroma to you and may it fill us with joy and hope. In Jesus' name, we pray, Amen.

PURE JOY

SCRIPTURE: James 1:2 NIV

"Consider it pure joy, my brothers and sisters, whenever you face trials of many kinds."

DECLARATION:

The author of James declares that we should consider it pure joy whenever we face trials of many kinds.

REFLECTION:

This passage can be difficult to understand at first glance. How can we possibly find joy in the midst of trials and difficulties? But as we reflect on it, we can begin to see that there is a deeper truth here. The joy that James speaks of is not a fleeting emotion based on our circumstances, but rather a deep-seated sense of peace and contentment that comes from knowing and trusting in God. When we face trials and difficulties, we are forced to rely on God in a way that we might not otherwise do. In these moments, we can experience the peace that comes from knowing that God is with us and that He will see us through.

MOTIVATION:

As we reflect on this passage, we are motivated to shift our focus from our circumstances to the God who is always with us. We are motivated to find joy in the midst of trials by trusting in God and relying on Him to see us through. We are also motivated to grow in our faith and become more like Christ through the challenges we face.

PRAYER:

Dear God, we thank you for the truth of your word. Help us to find joy in the midst of trials and difficulties by trusting in you and relying on your strength. May we grow in our faith through the challenges we face, and may we become more like Christ with each passing day. In Jesus' name, we pray., Amen.

REJOICE ALWAYS

SCRIPTURE: 1 Thessalonians 5:16-18 NIV
"Rejoice always, pray continually, give thanks in all circumstances; for this is God's will for you in Christ Jesus."

DECLARATION:

The author of 1Thessalonians declares that we should rejoice always, pray continually, and give thanks in all circumstances, for this is God's will for us in Christ Jesus.

REFLECTION:

In this passage, we are reminded of the importance of having a joyful and grateful heart in all circumstances. It's easy to be joyful and thankful when things are going well, but what about when we face challenges or difficulties? The truth is our circumstances don't determine our joy or gratitude. Rather, it is a choice that we make. When we choose to rejoice always, pray continually, and give thanks in all circumstances, we are able to experience God's peace and presence in a powerful way.

MOTIVATION:

As we reflect on this passage, we are motivated to choose joy and gratitude, no matter what we may be facing. We are motivated to cultivate a heart of prayer and to stay connected to God throughout our day. We are also motivated to trust in God's goodness and faithfulness, even when we can't see the way ahead.

PRAYER:

Dear God, we thank you for the gift of your presence in our lives. Help us to choose joy and gratitude in all circumstances, knowing that you are with us and that you are working all things for our good. May we cultivate a heart of prayer and stay connected to you throughout our day. In Jesus' name, we pray, Amen.

THIS IS THE DAY

SCRIPTURE: Psalm 118:24 NIV

"This is the day the Lord has made; let us rejoice today and be glad."

DECLARATION:

The psalmist declares that the day we are in is a day that the Lord has made, and we are called to rejoice and be glad in it.

REFLECTION:

This verse is a reminder that each day is a gift from God, and we are called to make the most of it. We don't always know what each day will bring, but we can trust that God is with us and that He has a plan for our lives. When we focus on the present moment and choose to rejoice and be glad in it, we are able to experience God's presence and peace in a powerful way.

MOTIVATION:

As we reflect on this verse, we are motivated to approach each day with a sense of gratitude and purpose. We are motivated to trust in God's plan for our lives and to make the most of every opportunity. We are also motivated to seek out ways to serve and bless others, knowing that each day is a gift that we can use to make a positive impact on the world around us.

PRAYER:

Dear God, we thank you for the gift of this day. Help us to approach each day with a sense of gratitude and purpose, knowing that you are with us and that you have a plan for our lives. May we rejoice and be glad in each moment, and may we use this day to serve and bless others. In Jesus' name, we pray, Amen.

INEXPRESSIBLE AND GLORIOUS JOY

SCRIPTURE: 1 Peter 1:8-9 NIV

"Though you have not seen him, you love him; and even though you don't see him now, you believe in him and are filled with an inexpressible and glorious joy, for you are receiving the end result of your faith, the salvation of your souls."

DECLARATION:

Peter declares that even though we have not seen Jesus, we can love him and believe in him, and as a result, experience an inexpressible and glorious joy. This joy comes from our faith and leads to the salvation of our souls.

REFLECTION:

As Christians, we are called to live a life of faith and trust in Jesus, even though we have not seen him with our physical eyes. This can be challenging at times, especially when we face difficult circumstances or when we see suffering and injustice in the world around us. But even in the midst of these challenges, we can experience a deep and abiding joy that comes from knowing Jesus and being saved by his grace.

MOTIVATION:

This passage is a powerful reminder that our faith in Jesus is not just a set of beliefs, but a source of joy and hope that sustains us in all circumstances. When we focus on our relationship with Jesus and the salvation that he offers us, we can experience a joy that is beyond words. This joy gives us the strength and courage to face whatever challenges come our way and to share the good news of Jesus with others.

PRAYER:

Heavenly Father, we thank you for the inexpressible and glorious joy that comes from knowing Jesus and being saved by his grace. Help us to keep our eyes fixed on him, even in the midst of difficult circumstances or trials. May our faith in Jesus lead us to a deeper sense of joy and hope that overflows into every aspect of our lives. In Jesus' name, we pray, Amen.

CHEERFUL HEART

SCRIPTURE: Proverbs 17:22 NIV

"A cheerful heart is good medicine, but crushed spirit dries up the bones."

DECLARATION:

The writer of Proverbs declares that a cheerful heart is good medicine. This implies that there is a healing power in having a positive and joyful attitude.

REFLECTION:

In our daily lives, we encounter many challenges and difficult situations that can easily lead us to feel discouraged and downhearted. However, this verse reminds us that having a cheerful heart can be a powerful antidote to these negative feelings. A positive attitude can help us to stay optimistic, find joy in the little things, and focus on the good things that are happening in our lives.

MOTIVATION:

This verse is a call to cultivate a cheerful heart, even in the midst of difficult circumstances. It reminds us that our attitude is a powerful tool that can help us to overcome obstacles, maintain healthy relationships, and find joy and contentment in our lives. By choosing to have a cheerful heart, we can experience the healing power of joy and positive.

PRAYER:

Dear God, help us to cultivate a cheerful heart, even in the midst of difficult circumstances. Give us the strength and courage to maintain a positive attitude, even when things are challenging. May we find joy and contentment in you and may that joy overflow into every aspect of our lives, bringing healing and hope to those around us. In Jesus' name, we pray, Amen.

CHEERFUL GIVER

SCRIPTURE: 2 Corinthians 9:7 NIV

"Each of you should give what you have decided in your heart to give, not reluctantly or under compulsion, for God loves a cheerful giver."

DECLARATION:

The Apostle Paul declares that God loves a cheerful giver. This implies that giving should be done with joy and a willing heart, rather than being forced or done out of obligation.

REFLECTION:

In our lives, we often struggle with giving, whether it be giving of our time, resources, or money. It can be easy to feel reluctant or hesitant to give, especially when we feel like we don't have enough for ourselves. However, this verse reminds us that giving should be done with joy and a willingness to bless others. God desires for us to give freely, not out of obligation or pressure.

MOTIVATION:

This verse is a call to become cheerful givers, to give with joy and gratitude, and to trust that God will provide for our needs. Giving should not be done begrudgingly, but with a spirit of generosity and a heart that desires to bless others. When we give cheerfully, we not only bless those around us, but we also experience the joy and satisfaction of being a part of God's work in the world.

PRAYER:

Dear God, help us to become cheerful givers, to give with joy and a willingness to bless others. Give us generous hearts and teach us to trust in your provision. May our giving reflect your love and grace in our lives. We pray that you would use our gifts to bring about your kingdom on earth and to bless those in need. In Jesus' name, we pray, Amen.

WELLS OF SALVATION

SCRIPTURE: Isaiah 12:3 NIV

"With joy you will draw water from the wells of salvation."

DECLARATION:

The prophet Isaiah declares that those who have received salvation will draw water with joy from the wells of salvation. This imagery depicts the abundance and life-giving nature of salvation that satisfies our deepest thirst.

REFLECTION: In our lives, we often search for fulfillment and satisfaction in various things, such as success, relationships, or material possessions. However, these things are fleeting and do not truly satisfy our deepest longings. Only God can truly satisfy our souls, and salvation through Jesus Christ who provides us with the ultimate source of fulfillment and joy. This verse reminds us that salvation is like a well that never runs dry. It is a source of life, renewal, and hope that we can draw from daily. When we drink from the wells of salvation, we experience joy, peace, and a sense of purpose that cannot be found in anything else.

MOTIVATION:

As believers, we are called to live our lives drawing from the wells of salvation with joy and gratitude. We are invited to live in the abundant life that Jesus offers us, to seek Him first and to find our satisfaction in Him. When we priorities our relationship with God and seek Him above all else, we experience the true fulfillment and joy that our souls long for.

PRAYER:

Dear God, thank you for the wells of salvation that satisfy our deepest thirsts. Help us to draw from them with joy and gratitude, knowing that only in you can we find true fulfillment and satisfaction. May we live our lives centred on you and seek you above all else, trusting that you will provide for all our needs. Jesus' name, we pray, Amen.

MY HEART TRUSTS IN HIM

SCRIPTURE: Psalm 28:7 NIV

"The Lord is my strength and my shield; my heart trusts in him, and he helps me. My

heart leaps for joy, and with my song I praise him."

DECLARATION:

The psalmist confidently declares that his heart trusts in God, and that he has been helped by Him. He acknowledges God as his strength, shield, and saviour.

REFLECTION:

Trusting in God is not always easy, especially during times of trouble or uncertainty. But when we place our trust in Him, we find strength and comfort. We can rely on God's unwavering faithfulness and know that He will never abandon us. As the psalmist says, when we trust in God, we can be confident that He will help us.

MOTIVATION:

Let us be encouraged to trust in God with our whole hearts, even when circumstances are difficult. When we do, we will find that He is faithful and will help us through every situation. We can take comfort in knowing that our God is strong and mighty, and that He will always be there to protect and guide us.

PRAYER: Heavenly Father, we come before You today and declare that our hearts trust in You. We thank You for being our strength, our shield, and our Saviour. Help us to always remember that You are with us, even in the most difficult times. We ask that You continue to guide and protect us and help us to grow in our faith and trust in You. In Jesus' name, Amen.

BLESSED ARE THOSE WHO KEEP HIS STATUTES

SCRIPTURE: Psalm 119:1-3 NIV

"Blessed are those whose ways are blameless, who walk according to the law of the Lord. Blessed are those who keep to his statutes and seek him with all their heart—they do no wrong but follow his ways."

DECLARATION:

The psalmist begins with a declaration of the blessedness of those who keep God's statutes and seek Him with their whole heart. He recognizes the importance of following God's commands and living a righteous life.

REFLECTION:

Keeping God's statutes and seeking Him with our whole heart is a sign of our love for Him. When we follow His commands, we are blessed with peace, joy, and a closer relationship with Him. The psalmist recognizes that living a righteous life requires discipline and effort, but the rewards are great.

MOTIVATION:

Let us be motivated to seek God with our whole heart and to keep His statutes. When we do, we will experience the blessings of a life lived in obedience to Him. We can trust that God's commands are for our good and that He desires the best for us. As we follow Him, we will grow in our love for Him and our desire to please Him.

PRAYER:

Heavenly Father, we thank You for Your statutes and commands. Help us to seek You with our whole heart and to live a righteous life. Give us the discipline and strength we need to follow Your commands and to trust that Your ways are best. May we experience the blessings of a life lived in obedience to You. In Jesus' name, Amen.

BLESSED ARE THOSE WHO KEEP MY WAYS

SCRIPTURE: Proverbs 8:32-35 NIV

"Now then my children, listen to me; blessed are those who keep to my ways. Listen to my instruction and be wise; do not disregard it. Blessed are those who listen to me, watching daily at my doors, waiting at my doorway. For those who find me find life and receive favour from the Lord."

DECLARATION:

In Proverbs 8:32-35, Wisdom personified calls out to those who will listen, inviting them to heed her ways and receive the blessings that come with it. For those who find me find life. Come to Jesus and live.

REFLECTION: God's wisdom is not just about knowledge or understanding, but it also involves action - keeping God's ways. The wisdom of God leads us to a life of righteousness, obedience, and blessings. When we follow God's ways, we are blessed with His favour, protection, and guidance.

MOTIVATION:

Let us be motivated to seek God's wisdom and to keep His ways. Let us be intentional in applying His wisdom to our daily lives, making choices that honour Him and bless us. When we choose to follow God's ways, we position ourselves to experience His favour, protection, and blessings.

PRAYER:

Dear God, we thank You for Your wisdom and guidance. Help us to seek Your ways and to keep them, that we may experience the blessings You have for us. Give us the strength and wisdom to make choices that honour You and bring blessings into our lives. May we find favour in Your sight as we follow Your ways. In Jesus' name, Amen.

WELL, DONE GOOD AND FAITHFUL SERVANT

SCRIPTURE: Matthew 25:23 NIV

"His master replied, 'Well done, good and faithful servant! You have been faithful with a few things; I will put you in charge of many things. Come and share your master's happiness!"

DECLARATION:

This is a statement of approval and commendation from the master in the parable of the talents. The master praises the servant who used his talents wisely and doubled them, showing that he was trustworthy and faithful.

REFLECTION:

As followers of Christ, we are all given talents and abilities, and it is our responsibility to use them for His glory. This parable reminds us that our faithfulness and diligence in using what God has given us will be rewarded. It is not enough to simply receive God's blessings; we must also be good stewards of them and use them to further His kingdom.

MOTIVATION:

Let us strive to be like the servant in the parable who used his talents wisely and doubled them, so that when we stand before our Master, we too may hear the words, "Well done, good and faithful servant." May we not be afraid to take risks and step out in faith to use our talents for His glory.

PRAYER:

Dear God, thank You for the talents and abilities You have given us. Help us to use them wisely and faithfully for your glory. Give us the courage to step out in faith and take risks to further your kingdom. May we hear Your words of approval and commendation, "Well done, good and faithful servant," when we stand before You. In Jesus' name, Amen.

LATTER RAIN

SCRIPTURE: Joel 2:23 NIV

"Be glad, people of Zion, rejoice in the Lord your God, for he has given you the autumn rains because he is faithful. He sends you abundant showers, both autumn and spring rains, as before."

DECLARATION:

We should rejoice each day knowing our God is faithful no matter what the season. When we know God, we have his Holy Spirit within us to face whatever comes our way.

REFLECTION:

The "latter rain" is a metaphor used in the Bible to describe the final outpouring of the Holy Spirit before the second coming of Jesus Christ. It is a time of spiritual refreshing and empowerment for believers, a time when God will pour out His Spirit in a special way to prepare His people for the great harvest of souls. Joel 2:23 speaks of the blessings that come with the "latter rain" - abundant showers that bring life and nourishment to the land. In the same way, the "latter rain" of the Holy Spirit brings new life and growth to the hearts of believers, enabling them to bear fruit for God's kingdom.

MOTIVATION:

As we await the "latter rain" of the Holy Spirit, we can prepare ourselves by seeking a deeper relationship with God, by studying His Word, by praying for His guidance and direction, and by being open to the leading of His Spirit in our lives. We can also pray for a greater outpouring of the Holy Spirit on our families, our communities, and our world, that many may come to know the love and saving grace of Jesus Christ.

PRAYER:

Heavenly Father, we thank you for the promise of the "latter rain" - for the outpouring of Your Spirit that will bring new life and growth to our hearts and to the hearts of those around us. Help us to prepare ourselves for this blessing by seeking You with all our hearts, by studying Your Word, by praying for Your guidance and direction, and by being open to the leading of Your Spirit in our lives. We also pray for a greater outpouring of Your Spirit on our families, our communities, and our world, that many may come to know the love and saving grace of Jesus Christ. In His name we pray, Amen.

DO NOT LET YOUR HEART BE TROUBLED

SCRIPTURE: John 14:1 NIV

"Do not let your hearts be troubled. You believe in God; believe also in me."

DECLARATION:

Jesus speaks to his disciples and comforts them with the assurance that they need not be troubled or afraid.

REFLECTION:

Life is full of uncertainty and challenges that can easily make our hearts troubled and fearful. In such moments, it's easy to feel overwhelmed and wonder how things will turn out. But Jesus reminds us that even in the midst of uncertainty, we can find peace in him. He calls us to trust him and not allow our hearts to be troubled. He knows that life can be hard, but he also knows that we can find hope and comfort in him.

MOTIVATION:

It can be easy to get caught up in our worries and fears, but we are called to trust in God's plan for our lives. When we face difficult situations, we can choose to focus on our fear or to trust that God is in control. We can choose to allow our hearts to be troubled or to find peace in him.

PRAYER:

Dear God, please help us to trust in You when life gets difficult. Help us to remember that You are always with me, even in the midst of uncertainty. Help us to find peace in You and not let our hearts be troubled. Amen.

REJOICE ALWAYS

SCRIPTURE: Philippians 4:4 NIV

"Rejoice in the Lord always. I will say it again: Rejoice!"

DECLARATION:

The Bible encourages us to rejoice always, regardless of our circumstances. In Philippians 4:4, it says "Rejoice in the Lord always. I will say it again: Rejoice!" This is a powerful reminder that joy is not dependent on our external circumstances, but rather on our relationship with God.

REFLECTION:

It can be challenging to find joy when we are faced with difficult situations, but God calls us to rejoice always. This means that even in the midst of trials, we can choose to focus on the goodness of God and find joy in His presence. We can remember that God is with us, and that He is faithful to see us through every situation.

MOTIVATION:

As believers, we have the Holy Spirit within us, who is the source of our joy. We can tap into this joy by spending time in prayer, worship, and reading the Word of God. When we focus on God's goodness and faithfulness, we can experience a deep sense of joy that transcends our circumstances.

PRAYER:

Heavenly Father, we thank You for the joy that You have given us through Your Spirit. Help us to remember to rejoice always, even in difficult times. Help us to focus on Your goodness and faithfulness, and to find joy in Your presence. Thank You for your love and faithfulness in our lives. In Jesus' name, Amen.

SHOUT FOR JOY

SCRIPTURE: Psalm 100:1-2 NIV

"Shout for joy to the Lord, all the earth. Worship the Lord with gladness; come before him with joyful songs."

DECLARATION: The Psalmist invites us to shout for joy to the Lord and to worship Him with gladness and gratitude.

REFLECTION:

It is easy to get caught up in the challenges and stresses of life and forget to focus on the blessings and goodness of God. However, the Psalmist reminds us that worship is not just about singing songs, but it is also about expressing joy and gratitude to the Lord for all He has done for us. When we choose to shout for joy to the Lord, we acknowledge His faithfulness and goodness in our lives, we seek an attitude of thanksgiving, love and peace that transforms our lives.

MOTIVATION:

Let us make a conscious effort to cultivate a lifestyle of worship that includes shouting for joy to the Lord. As we express our gratitude and joy, we invite the presence of the Lord into our lives, and we experience His peace and comfort. Let us not allow the challenges of life to rob us of our joy, but instead, let us choose to focus on the goodness of God and shout for joy to Him.

PRAYER:

Dear Lord, we come before You with grateful hearts, and we choose to shout for joy to You. Help us to cultivate a lifestyle of worship that includes expressing our joy and gratitude to You. May our worship bring glory to Your name, and may we experience Your presence and peace in our lives. Amen.

FULLNESS OF JOY

SCRIPTURE: Psalm 16:11

"You make known to me the path of life; you will fill me with joy in your presence, with eternal pleasures at your right hand."

DECLARATION:

I declare that in the presence of God, there is fullness of joy, and I choose to embrace and experience this joy in every aspect of my life.

REFLECTION:

This verse penned by king David reveals a profound truth about our relationship with God. In His presence, we can find a joy that surpasses all understanding and a satisfaction that cannot be found anywhere else.

The concept of "fullness of joy" speaks of a joy that is complete, abundant, and lacking nothing. It is not a fleeting happiness dependent on external circumstances but a deep-rooted sense of contentment that flows from being in the presence of the Almighty. This joy is not limited to specific moments or seasons; it is a continuous and ever-present beautiful gift from our loving Creator.

MOTIVATION:

In a world that is often filled with trials, disappointments, and uncertainties, it is easy to become overwhelmed and lose sight of joy. However, as followers of Christ, we are called to live differently. We have been invited into an intimate relationship with our heavenly Father, who longs to share His joy with us. God's desire is for us to experience His presence and allow His joy to permeate every aspect of our lives.

Choosing to embrace the fullness of joy in God's presence is a conscious decision we can make daily. It requires a shift in our perspective, focusing on His goodness rather than our circumstances. When we fix our eyes on Him, we begin to see beyond the temporary challenges and find solace in His eternal promises.

PRAYER:

Dear Heavenly Father, thank You for the gift of Your presence and the promise of fullness of joy that it brings. Help us to continually seek You, to set our hearts and minds on things above. Lord, in those moments when we are tempted to despair or be consumed by the difficulties of life, remind us of the abounding joy available to us in Your presence. Teach us to find contentment in You alone and to trust that Your plans for our lives are good. May our lives reflect the joy that comes from knowing and walking with you. In Jesus' name, we pray. Amen.

IN THE MULTITUDE OF MY ANXIETIES

SCRIPTURE: Psalm 94:19. *NIV*

"When anxiety was great within me, your consolation brought me joy".

DECLARATION: In the midst of my overwhelming anxieties and troubles, I will find solace in the unfailing love of God.

REFLECTION:

Life is filled with uncertainties, trials, and challenges that often leave us feeling anxious and burdened. We encounter moments when our hearts are heavy, and our minds are filled with worries and fears. It is during these times that we need to remind ourselves of the comforting words found in this Psalm 94:19: *"When anxiety was great within me, your consolation brought me joy".*

The psalmist acknowledges the reality of his many anxieties, recognizing the weight they carry in his heart. We, too, can relate to this sentiment, as we navigate the complexities of life. However, what sets the psalmist's perspective apart is his unwavering faith in God's comforting presence.

MOTIVATION:

When our anxieties multiply within us, it is easy to become overwhelmed and discouraged. We may feel as though we are drowning in a sea of worry, unable to find relief or peace. But in the midst of our distress, we can find solace in the unchanging character of our loving God.

God's comforts are not temporary or fleeting; they are a balm to our weary souls. He offers a peace that surpasses all understanding, assuring us that we are not alone in our struggles. Through His presence, He speaks words of encouragement, hope, and restoration into our lives. His love envelops us, providing a sanctuary of comfort in the midst of life's storms.

PRAYER:

Dear Heavenly Father, we come before You today with a heavy heart, burdened by the multitude of anxieties that weigh us down. Lord, we confess that at times we feel overwhelmed and helpless in the face of life's challenges. But we thank You for the assurance that Your comforting presence is always with us. In the midst of our anxieties, we ask for Your peace that surpasses all understanding. Help us to cast our cares upon You, knowing that You care deeply for us. Renew our spirits and restore our souls, as we find solace in Your unfailing love. May Your comforts delight our hearts, bringing us the assurance that You are in control, and we are held securely in Your hands. Grant us the strength to persevere through the trials we face, knowing that You are our refuge and strength. Help us to trust in Your perfect timing and Your sovereign plan for our lives. As we seek Your face, may Your comforting presence guide and fill us with renewed hope. In Jesus' name, we pray. Amen.

I HAVE SET THE LORD

ALWAYS BEFORE ME.

Scripture Psalm 16:8 NIV

"I keep my eyes always on the Lord. With him at my right hand, I will not be shaken".

DECLARATION:

In every step I take, in every decision I make, and in every circumstance, I face, I choose to set the Lord always before me.

REFLECTION:

Psalm 16:8 beautifully captures the essence of a life anchored in the presence of God. It speaks of a conscious decision, an intentional act of positioning ourselves in alignment with the divine. It is a declaration of unwavering faith and an acknowledgment of the trans formative power of God's presence in our lives.

MOTIVATION:

Life often presents us with countless distractions, uncertainties, and trials that threaten to unsettle us. However, when we set the Lord always before us, we establish a firm foundation upon which to build our lives. It is a deliberate choice to fix our gaze on the eternal rather than being consumed by the temporal. In setting the Lord always before us, we acknowledge His sovereignty, wisdom, and faithfulness. We recognise that He is the source of true joy, guidance, and purpose. With this perspective, we are able to navigate the challenges and triumphs of life with a steadfast spirit, knowing that God is with us every step of the way.

PRAYER:

Heavenly Father, we come before You today with a heart filled with gratitude and a desire to align our lives with Your divine purpose. We declare that we will set You always before us, placing You at the centre of our thoughts, decisions, and actions. Help us, Lord, to continually seek Your presence and to find our refuge in You. In moments of doubt and confusion, remind us of Your unwavering love and unchanging faithfulness. Empower us to walk in the confidence that comes from knowing You are with us, guiding our steps and leading us in the paths of righteousness. Grant us the wisdom to discern Your will and the strength to follow it faithfully.

May Your presence be a constant source of joy, peace, and comfort in our lives. We surrender ourselves to Your divine plan, trusting that as we set You always before us, our lives will be a testament to Your glory. May we walk each day with the Lord ever before us, finding solace and peace in His presence, and experiencing the fullness of His joy and blessing. In Jesus' name, we pray. Amen.

SPLENDOUR

SCRIPTURE: 1 Chronicles 16:27 NIV

"Splendour and majesty are before him; strength and joy are in his dwelling place."

DECLARATION:

Today, I declare that I will embrace the splendour of God's presence in my life. I will seek Him diligently and allow His glory to transform me from within.

REFLECTION:

1 Chronicles 16:27 paints a vivid picture of the awe-inspiring presence of God. His splendour refers to His magnificent beauty, radiance, and greatness. It is a splendour that surpasses anything we can comprehend or imagine. As we meditate on this verse, we are reminded of the privilege we have to enter into the dwelling place of the Almighty. In His presence, we find strength to face the challenges of life, and joy that transcends our circumstances. It is a dwelling place filled with love, grace, and peace.

MOTIVATION:

The splendour of God's presence is available to each one of us. It is not reserved for a select few but is extended to all who seek Him wholeheartedly. God invites us to draw near to Him, to bask in the brilliance of His glory, and to experience His transforming power. Let us be motivated to pursue God passionately, knowing that in His presence, our lives are forever changed. When we seek Him with all our hearts, we discover the depth of His love and the abundance of His blessings. Our lives become a reflection of His splendour as we walk in alignment with His will.

PRAYER:

Heavenly Father, we are in awe of Your splendour and majesty. Thank You for inviting us into Your presence and for making strength and joy available to us. Today, we surrender our hearts to You completely. Help us seek You diligently and wholeheartedly. Transform us from the inside out and make our lives a reflection of Your splendour. Fill us with Your strength and joy as we walk in obedience to Your Word. May we continually seek God's splendour and find our strength and joy in Your presence. May Your glory shine through our lives, impacting those around us and drawing them closer to You. In Jesus' name, we pray. Amen.

APPRECIATION

Thanks to Colin Mackenzie my husband for his, love and support, and wonderful photographs taken in different parts of the UK Thanks to Nikki Love for her help, formatting, layout, and suggestions while making this devotional book.

ABOUT THE AUTHOR

My name is Cindy Mackenzie and when I was 15, I believe God told me I would marry a minister. When I met Colin, he worked in Woolworths! When he asked me to marry him, I told him I really believed I would marry a minister. However, as I prayed, I knew Colin was for me. It was many years later that he told me he knew God was calling him into ministry. We both cried as we realised God was in control of everything. God gave me a heart for evangelism, and I have had the privilege of leading many people to Christ. Colin and I make a great team and we are so happy to have a marriage which is God centred. Of course, we have had our ups and downs nothing is perfect but being able to say sorry and pray seeking

God's help and wisdom has helped us to keep on going and serving the Lord together. Lord. May God bless you as you read these devotions and spend time with Him. My prayer is you will grow in your faith and be the person God created you to be. I have several more books coming, so follow me on Facebook to keep up to date. Some of my favourite photos Colin has taken are in this book.

Every Blessing, Cindy

Footnote

If you want to join my Facebook page type in Cindy Mackenzie Ministries, where you will find me.
https://www.facebook.com/groups/20693735 9421178

To see Colin's photo vlogs, go to:

www.youtube.com/@colinmackenziephotograp hy9009

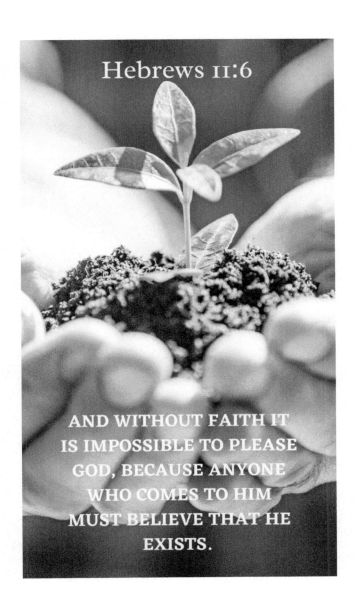

Hebrews 11:6

AND WITHOUT FAITH IT
IS IMPOSSIBLE TO PLEASE
GOD, BECAUSE ANYONE
WHO COMES TO HIM
MUST BELIEVE THAT HE
EXISTS.

Printed in Great Britain
by Amazon